NO EXCUSES *GET IT DONE.*

THIS BOOK WILL TEACH YOU HOW TO MASTER YOUR MINDSET AND CONQUER MENTAL PARALYSIS

ROCKY J. TURNER

AUSTIN
BROTHERS PUBLISHING

No Excuses - Get It Done

Rocky Turner

Published by Austin Brothers Publishing, Fort Worth, Texas

www.abpbooks.com

ISBN 978-1-7324846-2-7

Printed in the United States of America

2023 -- Second Edition

I WRITE DOWN EVERYTHING, AND I CHALLENGE YOU TO DO THE SAME. I'VE PROVIDED YOU WITH SEVERAL BLANK PAGES AT THE END OF THIS BOOK FOR YOU TO START WRITING DOWN YOUR CREATIVE IDEAS, GOALS OR ANY RANDOM POSITIVE THOUGHT THAT POPS IN YOUR HEAD. IF YOU ARE LIKE ME, THESE BLANK PAGES WILL FILL UP FAST. MAKE SURE YOU PURCHASE A NOTEPAD AND KEEP WITH YOU EVERYWHERE YOU GO. I HIGHLY RECOMMEND GETTING A *PASSION PLANNER*. IN MY OPINION, THE *PASSION PLANNER* IS ONE OF THE BEST DAILY, WEEKLY, MONTHLY AND YEARLY ORGANIZERS ON THE MARKET, PLUS IT HAS LOTS OF BLANK PAGES FOR NOTE TAKING.

EFFECTIVE NOTE TAKING helps you to remember information and aids your understanding of that information. Once created, your notes then act as a record of your thinking and they also provide the source material for your next creative or business project.

Contents

Life Mission Statement

Be a Catalyst for Positive Change in the lives of Others.

Signature Quotes

"If You Take Short Cuts, You will get Cut Short!"

"Me, Helping You be a better You....
Makes Me a better Me."

"Helping Others Achieve Greatness are the results of
You being Great."

Life Motto

NO EXCUSES, GET IT DONE!

Introduction

What is the first thing that pops into your mind whenever you are determined to move forward? A positive or negative thought? Whatever it is, it can control you and throw you into an ecstatic frenzy or mental paralysis.

Recently, people are starting to wake up to the truth about growth. Many people have taken several journeys to find the truth and determine what success and growth in life really mean. If you are holding this book in your hands, it clearly indicates that you are interested in prioritizing your success in the most ideal manner. It also means that you are willing to discover the different things you can do differently to connect with your growth.

You are on your way to becoming more certain of what you want to choose out of life and also what you are willing to give back to it.

Pause for a while, and take a deep breath. This could be the only reason you need to push harder and the life-changing opportunity you might want to take advantage of.

This book, in large part, is written for your consumption. It is a MUST-READ as it will provide you with all the necessary tools you need to configure your mind, how to escape mental paralysis, some skills needed to navigate through the struggle, and how to stay committed to and trust the process. It teaches you how to be a better version of yourself, how to rise and break barriers regardless of the limitations while pursuing your dream, your God-given purpose for your life.

My Story

Remember, when you're a kid, and people frequently ask, "What do you want to be when you grow up?" I had two goals, and they never changed—I wanted to be a professional athlete and a Radio DJ. I latched on to that dream early, and it stayed with me through school and never left me until I accomplished both. Let me explain how that happened.

I was born in Detroit and raised in Dallas. I had two sets of friends. One group played sports, made good grades in school, and was a positive influence in my life. The other set were gang bangers, school dropouts, and drug dealers—bad influences. I tried hard to satisfy both sets of friends because I didn't want anyone to think I wasn't cool. I was cool with everyone. The first time I realized that one bad choice could ruin your life was when one of my "Bad Influence" friends was tragically shot. I wasn't with this group of friends on that particular night, but that bullet could have struck me if I had been. It takes something like that for a young man to realize he's not indestructible.

The second "WAKE UP CALL" in my life was when I received an F on my report card. Texas had a rule called "No Pass, No Play," which meant if you didn't pass all your classes, then you couldn't participate in extra-curricular activities, including sports. SPORTS was the one thing that helped keep me out of trouble. These two experiences scared me, and I made a promise to God, my parents, teachers, coaches, and anyone else who had a positive influence on my life that I was going to focus on achieving my goals and inspiring others to do the same.

From that day on, I worked hard, harder than most. I rolled up my sleeves, buckled down, made the honor roll at school, and earned a baseball scholarship to college. The baseball scholarship was interesting. It was to Ranger Junior College in the small town of Ranger, Texas population of less than 3,000 people. It wasn't the pinnacle of the baseball world, but I worked hard to get there. Actually, I turned down a scholarship to play football at Texas Tech University.

Let me tell you how that happened. My development as an athlete was slower than most, especially in baseball. In middle school, I was on the B-team in football, but I was convinced I belonged on the A-team. The knock was that I was not fast enough and too skinny. However, I wasn't discouraged. I kept busting my butt and constantly telling MYSELF that I was good enough.

I have always been an overachiever. However, it was the JOURNEY of the struggle that strengthened me and made me who I am today. I learned at an early age to embrace struggle and adversity. When anything negative came my way, I learned to find the POSITIVE within. It made me stronger, and I knew that one day I would get my shot.

My status didn't change when I arrived at Arlington High School. It was still obvious that physically I wasn't yet ready for the big time. This time I allowed the adversity to get the best of me. I quit caring, and my grades slipped. After failing another class, I missed a half year of football because of being ineligible. My coaches couldn't depend on me, but I've always had the heart of a lion.

Finally, by the time of my Junior year, I earned a spot as starting wide receiver on Varsity. This was my shot, and

I wasn't about to lose it. Outworking everyone else was my mission, and it became a part of who I am. I was blessed to have good Junior and Senior year seasons and earned a scholarship to Texas Tech.

Meanwhile, back at the baseball field, I didn't start, nor did I play much. I was a sub, often nothing more than a pinch runner. It bothered me, but I kept working hard, again preparing for when I did get my shot. Although I was ready to accept the football scholarship to Texas Tech, I still wanted to prove myself as a baseball player. A pro baseball scout noticed me while playing in a summer baseball league and saw my raw talent. He encouraged me to attend a Junior College baseball program and have the opportunity to be selected in the Major League Baseball draft after my second year.

My older brother Andre, who was a great baseball player, challenged me to start training with him every day to help enhance my baseball skills. "IT WORKED." My Arm Strength improved, my hitting improved, and my confidence improved.

My Freshman and Sophomore years at Ranger Jr. College were very successful. I was excited about the upcoming MLB baseball draft, but it came and went, and my name was not selected.

However, I did receive a scholarship to play baseball at the University of Texas at Arlington (UTA) for my Junior and Senior seasons. Adversity hit once again. I never will forget this moment. Coach Butch McBroom, another phenomenal person who saw something special in me, pulled me aside and told me that he wanted me to be a switch-hitter. If you're not a baseball fan, that means batting both left and right-handed, depending on who's pitching. It's a valuable skill but not easy to develop. I gave it a try with little success.

The coach kept telling me not to worry, just keep at it. He frequently said, "You'll thank me later." About halfway through my Junior season, I got mad and told the coach I didn't want to switch-hit any longer. What I didn't know was that I was hurting myself because scouts saw my potential as a switch-hitter. At the beginning of my Senior year, Coach McBroom asked me to try again. I said, "No!" It was my last opportunity to have a good year and make an impression so I could play pro ball.

After getting off to a good start, I was convinced I had made the right choice. However, I fell into a huge slump. One afternoon I was approached by a scout who asked why I had stopped switch-hitting. He didn't accept my explanation and told me to persevere. He was confident I had the ability. I told the coach I would try again and finish the year strong.

On the day of the MLB draft after my Senior season, my phone rang. It was the same scout who initially told me after High School that if I worked hard, I would be drafted one day. He was right. I was selected by the New York Mets. Words can't tell you how grateful and excited I was. I quickly dropped to my knees and thanked God for making one of my childhood dreams of being a pro athlete come true.

As my baseball career progressed, I knew it was important to have other options because it wouldn't last forever. So, it was time to get serious about my second childhood dream of being a radio DJ. After my baseball career, I went to the #1 radio station in Dallas, Texas, at the time (K-104 FM) to apply for a job. I was turned down. Not once, but five times. I went back a sixth time and told them I would work FREE of charge, just to get my foot in the door. I offered to do whatever needed to be done. I just wanted permission to be there and learn the business. I really want this portion of my story to stick in your head. This was a defining NO EXCUSES GET IT DONE moment in my life.

K104 FM said "Yes" to my offer. Who can turn down people who will work for free? So the GRIND began. I provided assistance with every department: Promotions,

Programming, Engineering, Production, Street Team, Mail room, ran errands, and did everything they would allow me or ask me to do. I had lost my baseball income, and I wasn't getting paid by the radio station, so I went out and did what I frequently did when facing a tough decision or situation; I found mentors. I sought out people who were smarter than me and picked their brains.

One of those mentors was Ray Burris, a former Major League Baseball pitcher. He advised me to start a baseball academy and teach youth how to develop their baseball skills. He said I could be an inspiration to the kids and also earn a living since they would pay for the training. I started the academy with two kids, but it quickly grew, and I eventually had 35. They provided enough income that I could continue working with the radio station.

I worked free at the radio station for an entire year. When a position became available, they were almost forced to hire me. How could they turn me down after that kind of commitment? Basically, I created my own position. Skip Cheatem was my first boss in the radio business. My first official On-Air job was the 2 am - 5 am overnight shift.   In radio, that's the worst shift you can have because the fewest people are listening. I was so excited to finally be an On-Air Jock that I yelled and screamed when talking on the mic. My energy was bouncing around the room like a laser light show. The next day, Skip brought me into his office and bluntly declared that being on the air may not be the job for me. He made it clear that all the hollering and screaming was terrible.

I wasn't ready to give up on my dream, so I asked for one more chance. He graciously agreed. He told me to "get on the mic and do exactly what I tell you!" I followed his instructions, and I've been on the air ever since. At the time this book was published, I've been in the Radio-Television business for 23 Years.

Although I have been extremely blessed to build a Big Brand in Radio, I was actually Fired TWICE! It's not unusual to be fired by a radio station. It's kind of a standing joke that if you're in radio, then you know how to be fired. So, I didn't give up. I decided to make my brand more valuable in order to make it hard for any radio company to fire me again.

I taught myself how to DJ and started offering my FREE DJ services to all of the Night Clubs in the city. Of course, the majority of them said YES. I showed up at every DJ job with Break Dancers, Hip Hop Dancers, and Street Team members, all wearing Rock-T branded T-Shirts and Hats, ready to hit the dance floor when I started my DJ Sets.

Needless the say, That Strategy worked. I started setting up my DJ System in all of the popular inner-city neighborhood parks, creating block parties. I hosted the Hype High School Pep Rallies in all of the School Districts in the metroplex. Word got around pretty fast, and everyone wanted to hire me to DJ, Host, and Promote their events. Then I was asked to host a new TV Show called "DANCE CLUB 21", and that elevated my brand to a higher level.

Here is another very important lesson to learn from MY STORY! If you make enough NOISE, people will come to see what you are doing, and If they like what you are doing, they will want to work with you. This is exactly what started happening to me. It became a "Ripple Effect." Big Brands like McDonald's, AT&T, Metro PCS, and many more started hiring me and my company to promote their brands in the streets and help execute marketing campaigns.

It was around this time that I met Celebrity Comedian Rickey Smiley, who had just started his new Rickey Smiley Morning Radio Show. After He found out about my sports background, he asked me to join his show as the Sports Analyst. My answer was YES, and The Rest is history. At the time this book was published, The Rickey Smiley Morning Show aired in nearly 100 Markets Nationwide with over 8 Million Daily Listeners.

I've been blessed to start several more successful companies and brands along the way, but please do understand that I FAILED more than I succeeded throughout my journey. Let me STOP right here and change that word "FAILED" to what I like to call "LEARNED."

Rule #1 of having a NO EXCUSES GET IT DONE MINDSET is to understand that you either WIN or you LEARN! If you fail at anything, that doesn't mean that you are a FAILURE. It means that you LEARNED what to do or what NOT to do next time.

This is only a snapshot of my story. I would need to dedicate an entire book to tell the entire story, but I have shared enough to set the tone for this book. I have experienced lots of adversity and hit many brick walls during my life and career, and two things have always pushed me through and gotten me over the hump every time:

GOD

Having a NO EXCUSES GET IT DONE Mindset

I pray that you allow God to lead your life and understand that YOU can accomplish anything that you put your mind to. BELIEVE IT, and you can BE IT! PERIOD!!!! Today is the last day that you except MEDIOCRITY! This book is not for Mediocre Mindset Thinkers! If you are content with living a mediocre lifestyle, then close this book now and give it to someone who wants to be LEGENDARY!!!!

DO NOT START THE NEXT CHAPTER BEFORE YOU COMPLETE THE ASSIGNMENT BELOW.

Refuse to let the word "NO" make you quit. Flip that word around and turn on your "ON" switch. Identify three areas of your life in which your NO (Adversity) needs to become an ON

1._____

2._____

3._____

Plugging into a higher source, something that's greater than you. People who are better than you. Those who are doing what you want to do but at a higher level. These people are called "mentors." Identify two people which you will ask to intentionally become your mentors.

1._____

2._____

Take The "Promise Made" self-checklist.

I am making a promise to myself that I will push through any adversity and NEVER quit on myself.

Initial each promise you are willing to work towards and keep.

_____ I will never quit

_____ I will always have a mentor in my life

_____ I will submit to my mentor's advice

_____ I will stay positive even though times get difficult for me

_____ I will stay mentally sharp and keep my head in my dream

_____ I will be honest and stay true to my dream

_____ I will surround myself with friends that have a positive influence on my life

_____ I will not allow my circumstance to determine my future

Chapter One

Break Free from Mental Paralysis

FIRST, understand that a mindset breakdown is needed from time to time to shift your focus and ears to your growth potential. One of the biggest obstacles to achieving success is the combination of frustration, confusion, and impatience. These negative emotions can derail even the most well-crafted plans and goals on your success journey.

It's important to recognize when we're getting caught up in our own heads **and learn to break free from these patterns!** By doing so, you can gain the mental clarity and focus you need to take on your challenges with confidence and resilience. So It's crucial to be able to distinguish between what's true and what's not in the world of growth.

It's true that the need to get up, no matter how low you are, can be a real struggle. When you get caught up in overthinking and feel like you can't take action, it can be really tough to break free from that cycle. Many people suffer from this mental paralysis, and in the real sense, it arises when a multitude of thoughts and emotions vie for attention in your mind, causing a sense of overwhelm and confusion.

The good news is that there are steps you can take to break free from this cycle and regain control of your life.

As you read this book, you will learn many Tips and Tools that you can apply to all areas of your life. This is your PlayBook to success in Life: Career, Relationships, Money, Time, Health & Fitness, Personal Growth, etc....

Read and Re-Read this book until you consistently start using these New Habits. Step #1 for achieving any goal is to develop a **NO EXCUSES GET IT DONE** Mindset, which will become your solid foundation for success.

This is really practical; **High confidence, self-esteem, positive thinking, and a relaxed state of mind are found in the power-centered mindset**; When you're experiencing optimism and that "get out there and do it" attitude, you're operating from a place that's filled with positive energy. If you can spend the majority of your time in this area, you're going to be more relaxed, have more energy, and enjoy your life more, knowing you're moving in a clear direction. You're able to make clear choices and bond with the right people to enhance your social interactions. You won't be worrying about the future; you'll be too busy creating it. **Your power-based center is a life defined by confidence, high self-esteem, goal achievement, taking healthy risks, and taking responsibility for your actions and your life.**

Although people will come to tell you why you should stay paralyzed in your mentality and give room to mediocrity, circumstances will tell you, and your background will. But in this positive-based center, life is good and has a clear meaning and steadfast purpose. We all want to be in this place to succeed, stretch beyond our comfort zones [mental prisons], and live life to the fullest. So why is it so hard to get to this place, to stay there, and to stay strong and free of your fear? Whenever you're in a situation that challenges you to try something new or act in a way that you've never done before, you experience fear.

That's good. Having the fear of something is the first step in dealing with it.

There is a list of activities that preoccupies your mind when you plan to make changes to your life, and this is absolutely normal, but let's take a practical step in offloading that baggage. One major quote that rules my life is to **never invest in anything you don't understand! Learn, then make your decisions!**

DO NOT START THE NEXT CHAPTER BEFORE YOU COMPLETE THE ASSIGNMENT BELOW.

Once you can see clearly what you want and how to get it, the final step is making the commitment to GO! Develop a plan to become what you want to be in life. (Write down the ideas that are deep down in your heart, don't be afraid to identify them, they will shape you, direct you, and fulfill you) Learn how to listen and listen to learn.

My Goal

_____

_____

_____

_____

_____

_____

_____

_____

_____

_____

_____

Why do I want to accomplish this Goal?

_____

_____

_____

_____

_____

Does my goal help others? If so, how?

_____

_____

_____

_____

_____

What do you see, hear, smell, taste, and feel throughout this Goal?

_____

_____

Rocky Turner

_____

_____

_____

_____

_____

_____

Chapter Two

Get Your Mind Right

What's the secret to a stronger mind and increased success rate? While there's no magic trick to mental strength, did you know that, just like our bodies, we can train our minds to be stronger through practice?

The mind is the center of everything that goes on in your life. When you think about ideas or words, your mind evaluates them, and over time, they start to shape your beliefs, which shifts your world and energy. You must guard your mind and your thoughts and carefully scrutinize what you choose to hold on to as your belief system. The way you view life and respond to it is dependent on how you think. What I am saying, in essence, is: the mind controls what comes and goes away from us. However, you can be in control of your mind.

As you go on in life, your experiences and conversations with people can influence you. What you hold to be true about yourself and the circumstances around you; your belief holds a great part of your growth and success. There is mostly no physical or tangible evidence to show that what you believe is true. But what happens is that your beliefs manifest in your words, actions, and attitude to life.

This influence can be direct or indirect. The fact remains that life presents you with thoughts, perceptions, and ideas. What you have is the power of choice. You can choose what to believe or not. And, when you have believed in the efficacy of something, it strongly controls everything you do and become.

Some beliefs can have a negative impact on you, your growth, and your ability to perform certain tasks. Even things like money, your definition of success, and your relationship with the world around you. Negative thinking patterns can be a big contributor to mental paralysis. Challenge these thoughts by asking yourself if they're true. Often, they're not as true as they seem. **Why do you believe that you can't? Trust me, you really can.**

"CREATE YOUR OWN MENTAL MOVIE OF WHO YOU WANT TO BE!"

Equally, some beliefs can have a positive impact on how you view yourself.

Your perception of yourself and what you feel about your worth or value tends to be influenced by the belief formed in your interaction with your families, friends, and society during your formative age. You tend to look at yourself from your own perspectives, and this may either affect you positively or negatively, carrying on even into adulthood.

You can change your self-image by providing it with a new truth. Your "self-image" refers to the beliefs and opinions you hold about yourself. These beliefs can be deeply ingrained and affect how you think, feel, and behave. You can create your own mental movie of who you want to be by adopting a new and more positive way of thinking about yourself.

"For as he thinketh in his heart, so is he...."

The thoughts you have internally are what prevent you from moving forward and achieving what you want. That is why it is necessary to silence your inner voice, that little voice that, when you think of your goal, tells you: "It is impossible," "You will not be able to," "It is very difficult," "what are you going to do it for," "there is no time," "that's fine," "what if he says no?", and give you all the reasons why you don't even have to bother trying

Having negative thoughts is addictive. This is because the human mind tends to make scary things seem worse than they really are. So, we are almost always ready to run away or fight. This is how we react to everything, especially bad things, that happen in our lives.

When things don't go as planned, the first thing we want to do is either run away or face the problem without thinking or reflecting.

Negative thinking doesn't give us the freedom to figure out ways to deal with ideas that could hurt us. Instead, it traps us inside the impossible, and everything we do would be geared towards the impossible.

People with a positive outlook tend to handle tough scenarios in a way that shows persistence, determination, and calm. You have to be like this to reach your goals and dreams.

First of all, negative thinking changes how you look at your life and how you live it. If you don't think you have any value, you'll live your life in a way that doesn't have any worth. This is because you wouldn't do anything special to change your life or the lives of the people around you.

Also, if you think you can't do anything right, it will definitely show in your work. You're too tired to do things and stick with them. In fact, our minds are in charge of our lives. People often say that they are what they think. This is a fact. Several studies have shown that how we think is a very important factor in everything that happens to us, good or bad.

1. Rather than worry over a problem, actively think about solutions to the problem.
2. Whenever you are upset, take 10 minutes to determine the right thing to do before taking any action.
3. If you have negative thoughts, write them down on paper and throw the paper away. Repeat this every time you have a negative thought in your mind.

"You are today where your thoughts have brought you; you will be tomorrow where your thoughts take you."

DO NOT START THE NEXT CHAPTER BEFORE COMPLETING THE ASSIGNMENT BELOW.

Often times we get in our own way because of self-doubt and how we think. Write down five things you believe are in your way and keep you from achieving your Goal.

1. _____

2. _____

3. _____

4. _____

5. _____

Chapter 3

Secret Trick to Re-Organize Your BRAIN

Did you know that you can unlearn and learn new experiences, new ways to do things, and above all, create positive habits that encourage general well-being and improve productivity?

Basically, You typically become a master of what you practice. Example...

- If you want to be more compassionate, you need to act compassionately.

That's why honing these abilities through repeated exercise is essential for developing mental strength and making them second nature. Therefore, being mentally strong comes naturally.

As with any skill, repetition is the key to becoming an expert. For illustration, consider the sport of tennis or the art of piano playing. By practicing what we've learned over and over, we strengthen connections in the brain and eventually perform the task with less concentration, focus, and energy.

You'll get to the point where you can play tennis or piano without giving it any thought. It's as simple as that. It becomes second nature.

Now let's go deeper. The same is true of our thinking and feeling habits. For instance, if you frequently entertain angry thoughts, you will eventually develop an angry personality. The slightest discomfort will eventually cause you to explode in anger. On the other hand, positivity and happiness can be permanently encoded in the brain of someone who practices finding the silver lining and positive in everything on a regular basis. I practice this skill daily.

Just like we train our bodies to be stronger through consistent exercise, we can also train our minds to be stronger. **"Positive Thinking"** training is the process of focusing on positive thoughts and behaviors. By doing this, we can create a stronger and happier mind, allowing us to unlock our potential and live a more fulfilling life.

"You can change your self-image by providing it with a new truth."

"We only go or fail to go because of our imagination."

In case you are unaware, your brain is your skillset and the horsepower for every activity you engage in. How well do you apply it?

How well do you read daily?

How well do you repeatedly practice that skill set in a week?

How well do you repeat your daily task?

How well do you repeatedly affirm positive words to yourself?

The more you repeatedly engage in activities, the more it becomes unconscious and easier. Learn to be a repeater of actions!!

Rising above Mediocrity

The opposite of greatness is mediocrity. Each individual has a distinctive set of skills and experiences.

You can overcome your circumstances no matter where you were born or how much money your family had. You have options beyond just accepting life as it is. If you think you can't improve yourself, you're making a huge mistake. Everyone has a unique starting point. Some individuals are born into extreme wealth, while others are born into poverty. What matters is how you use the parts you've been dealt with. There will be winners and losers.

It's not how far you can reach for freedom but how far you're willing to reach. You'll never know how close you were to success if you quit now. Understand that you can't control what others do or say, and sometimes you can't control how you were raised, but you always have a choice in how you respond to it.

Your strength is yours to use in whatever way you see fit. You have the option of accepting your current situation as inevitable or remaining in the here and now and taking the necessary steps to improve your situation. Past mistakes, losses, and tragedies can never be undone. Your history is not your future, but your future might become your past if you dwell there.

When faced with adversity, individuals typically give up and settle for mediocrity. Don't just accept it. The only way to achieve greatness is to reject the acceptance of mediocrity. This is how you reach your fullest potential and make your life into the extraordinary journey God has in store for you.

To get past mediocrity, you need to develop skills and habits that the average person doesn't have. You must lift the lid on yourself and create momentum in your life by overcoming obstacles and scaling new heights. All creation has potential and the power to fulfill, but this can only be done by unleashing your potential.

You must develop habits and a culture from which you can channel positive energies.

Those who perceive themselves to be a "failure type person" will find some way to fail. You can only be average if you believe you are average.

DO NOT START THE NEXT CHAPTER BEFORE COMPLETING THE ASSIGNMENT BELOW

Habit -a settled or regular tendency or practice, especially one that is hard to give up.

Apply the **"What's the Positive Solution?"** to your life

1. Every time you hear or see anything negative, come up with an alternative positive solution.
2. Practice this exercise below. Write 5 Negative Situations and come up with a Positive Solution.

NEGATIVE:

1. _____

2. _____

3. _____

4. _____

5. _____

POSITIVE SOLUTION

1. _____

2. _____

3. _____

4. _____

5. _____

You don't have to broadcast this to everyone; keep it to yourself. This will help you rewire your mindset.

Just remember that ***Nobody can make you feel inferior without your permission.***

Chapter 5

FEAR is Not Real

"Fear is not real; it's a product of our imagination!"

Let's face it - we all have fears. Whether it's the fear of failure, the fear of rejection, or the fear of spiders, there's no escaping those pesky little anxieties that creep up on you when you least expect it.

"Failing at something does not mean that you are a failure. Failing means you have learned what to do or what not to do next time."

The fruit of everything good in life begins with a challenge. Going through the pain is part of the deal, and if you can't handle the pain, then you don't want success. You have to look at life when life knocks you down and ask; this is all you've got? Every time you run up against a trial and obstacle, don't stop! Instead, recycle your pain. Use your pain! Most times, it's not because you can't do it but because you can't outlast your old you to get your new you.

Can you give up your present reality in order to manifest your growth?

Are you ready to pick the baton?

Most people don't reach their goals because they give up. Not failure itself, but their first loss is what stops them. People who are successful don't give up after one mistake. Instead, they take responsibility and keep learning from their mistakes so they can do better next time. If you learn from the mistakes you make, you can only get better.

Failure makes the winner stronger. But it makes most people give up or feel like they aren't worth anything. Now, you have to decide if you are a winner or just a person. Winners hate failing, but they would never give up because of it. Every great thing on Earth was made because the person who made it learned from what worked and what didn't.

When you're a kid learning to ride a bike for the first time, you fall down a lot, but you get back up and keep trying until you get it. Failure isn't the end of your story; it's the start of your comeback story. If failure is the end of the story, there will be no great or wealthy people on Earth. Yes, you've failed, but now is the time to learn from your mistakes and even try harder to succeed. People who are successful today are where they are not because they never failed or had failures. Instead, they are where they are because they didn't stop when they failed. Instead, they built themselves up and made the failure a part of their past so they could get to where they are now. Your mistake should only teach you what not to do and how to do things better next time.

Here's the thing - when you let those fears control you, you're not doing yourself any favors.

You're essentially letting those fears hold us back from achieving our goals and being as productive as we can be.

"Live facing your fears or die tasting your tears!"

Well, the first step is acknowledging that those fears exist. It's like the kind of scene in "Finding Nemo" when Dory tells Marlin to "just keep swimming." You need to accept the fact that you are scared, and It's holding you down. Then reframe those fears in a positive way. For example, instead of fearing failure, you can view it as an opportunity to learn and grow. And instead of fearing rejection, you can see it as a chance to find a better fit. When you pursue worthy goals, you will encounter difficulties. To achieve your desired level of success, you must embrace your fears. If you mentally prepare yourself, these fears will vanish swiftly. Your mind will perceive that the obstacle has already been overcome. If you find it challenging to psych yourself up, repeat the process until your mind settles down and allows you to concentrate on what you want.

Another great way to deal with fears is to talk about them with a friend or colleague. Sometimes just putting those fears out into the open can help us realize that they're not as scary as we thought. Plus, it's always nice to have a supportive cheerleader in our corner! Embrace those fears, reframe them in a positive light, and keep on truckin'. Before you know it, you'll be a productivity machine!

"You either win or you "learn." You learn more from your failures vs. Your successes.

The next time you're feeling fearful, remember - you got this! You are going beyond your limit and making your fear powerless over your achievements, and you are definitely achieving your success!

Don't be afraid to start over again! You're not starting over from scratch; you are starting from experience!

I remember being offered an opportunity to join the DISH NATION TV Show on FOX. However, it was miles away from my family. This caused tension on how I would be able to keep that bond with the family and also earn for my family. The risk was so daring, but it eventually paid off. I was skeptical about keeping the job, but I knew opportunities like this are rare, and I am glad it made me who I am. There was doubt and fear at first, but I faced it head-on and realized I was in my own head. The best way to eliminate FEAR from your life is to have the COURAGE to face it!

DO NOT START THE NEXT CHAPTER UNTIL YOU COMPLETE THE ASSIGNMENT BELOW.

Most people never start because of fear or self-doubt. This exercise will surely help alleviate your fears by facing them head-on. You will be surprised by how basic these questions are and how they will be the starting point for making bold decisions. Indecision is exactly what breeds fear. So ask yourself this:

What is the source of your fear, and where does it come from?

_____

_____

Why are you Fearful? (Failure? Losing your job?)

_____

_____

What is the worst that could happen if you go after your goals?

_____

_____

What is the best that could happen if you go after your goals?

_____

_____

How real are those imagined fears?

_____

_____

Are you afraid of the process?

_____

_____

How secure are you with your ability? Do You believe in YOU?

_____

_____

Write down two names of people or mentors who support you and your goals. Feel free to add names to this list over time. These are your CHEERLEADERS who will help you eliminate FEAR and keep pushing toward your goals.

FEAR IS A GOOD THING WHEN YOU ARE NOT AFRAID TO FACE IT!

Chapter 6

Jump and the Net Will Appear

When faced with confusion, it's easy to get stuck in a state of mental paralysis. It makes you think too much about every choice, weighing the pros and cons and looking for the best solution. Obviously, taking risks can be terrifying. There is always the possibility that things will not go as planned. But when you let fear stop you, you stop yourself from growing and learning. When you don't leave your comfort zones, you limit your own potential and miss out on the amazing things that can happen.

When you jump and trust that a net will appear, you use your own inner strength and resilience. Even when you don't know what will happen, you know that you can build your own safety net. And when you take the first action, jump, you get the energy that can push you toward success.

Taking action despite your fears and doubts makes you more likely to take chances to reach your goals, no matter what happens. Think you can do it, take that first step, and keep going with faith and determination. You never know what amazing things might be waiting for you on the other side of that jump. However, this doesn't mean you should charge ahead recklessly. Instead, start small by choosing one area of your life where you're feeling stuck and making a commitment to take action on it today.

One step at a time!

You have to be fearless when it comes to achieving your goals. Nobody had the perfect manual before they got started, but one thing was certain, they started anyways!

You have to be extremely super confident in what you don't know!

Ask yourself;

- Will I regret not taking any steps toward my goals?
- Do my goals matter to me?
- Is my present activity synced with my goals?
- Are my choices getting me closer to my goals?

DON'T START THE NEXT CHAPTER UNTIL YOU COMPLETE THE ASSIGNMENT BELOW

- It's Time to pull out your Journal or Note Pad.
- Make a page with two columns.
- At the top of one column, write the word **"Positive."**
- Under the positive column, list the names of people you hang out with, family and friends, who encourage you in pursuit of your Dreams & Goals.
- At the top of the second column, write the word **"Negative."**
- On the negative column, list those people who discourage you or don't offer any positive reinforcement. Remember, this journal is only for your benefit and not to be shared, so be honest. The goal is not to cut these people off but to be more aware of who is helping you and who is not. Spend more time talking with and listening to the

ones in the positive column and less time listening to those in the negative column.

Your response will determine if you have what it takes to jump. At least, take a step toward your goal, start that business, pick up that book, start learning that skill, and be fierce about harnessing each opportunity.

Chapter 7

Don't Let Your Past Hold You Down

JUST DO IT! BE WILLING TO BE WRONG, SO YOU CAN DISCOVER WHAT IS RIGHT!

STOP WORRYING ABOUT WHY SOMETHING HAPPENED!

START FOCUSING ON WHAT YOU ARE GOING TO DO TO FIX IT!

Many people only want to do two things when they talk about the past. Either to forget the past or to think about it a lot. They don't care about what happened in the past because they are afraid of what happened there and can't look back on it. Or living in the past by letting their past control them and letting their past define them. In the end, their past will destroy their life and stop them from doing what they want to do. There is no clear way forward if you live in the past or forget about it. The smart way to be successful is to look at the past and figure out how to move forward and where to make changes. In the end, success comes from having the right tools and the right knowledge. If you don't learn from the past, you'll never be successful.

On your way to success, you need to know that you are expected to fail because failure is the first step toward success. This may not seem like it makes sense, but it does. Failure is a learning experience that makes you wiser and, in the end, a better version of yourself. Failure is one of the best ways to learn, and it is a great teacher.

FALL DOWN 9 TIMES, GET UP 10
SUCCESS IS ACCOMPLISHED BY LEARNING FROM YOUR
PAST ERRORS!

When you know about the past, you can see trends and tendencies. When you look back, you can start to see patterns in the choices you made and what happened as a result.

ADOPT A GPS MINDSET. DON'T BE AFRAID OF MISTAKES. WHEN YOU MAKE A WRONG TURN, IMMEDIATELY LEARN FROM IT, RE-CALIBRATE, AND GET BACK ON COURSE!

When you think about the past, it doesn't mean you should judge your present life based on what you did in the past. No, it's you who has learned from the past, chosen to be better, and succeeded despite having failed before. Then, if you fall or fail, figure out what went wrong and move on. The road in front of you is harder than what you went through down below.

One of the best ways to think about the past is to write in a book. Writing down your ideas and experiences can teach you a lot about yourself and how you act and think. You can also keep track of your progress over time and celebrate your wins as you go. Keeping a journal is a good way to think about your past wins and failures and to improve yourself.

Have Vision. You need to be goal-oriented or vision-ary if you want to be successful in life. Goals are aspirations with a time limit. If you're ready to say "no" to procrasti-nation, or you've hit rock bottom, and you want to rekin-dle your goals or visions, then you need to start aiming for the stars right now. In the words of acclaimed author Brian Tracy, your life will undergo a radical transformation if you are willing to push yourself outside your comfort zone.

Believe. You need a firm conviction in yourself to push yourself beyond your comfort zone while aiming for the stars." Belief is an attitude, a point of view, or the way you think about something. What you learn and experi-ence influences your beliefs and values. Motivating your-self to alter your outlook is the first step. If you have faith in yourself, you will develop an optimistic attitude no matter who you are, how much schooling you've had, or where you find yourself in life.

Believing in something means believing in its possi-bilities. We can thus infer that not believing in something is the same as not believing it is possible.

Be innovative. Having a plan and some ideas in mind will also help. Every success, great or small, starts with an idea. Ideas, not money, are what really make a company successful. While there is no shortage of ideas, there is a shortage of those with the creativity and innovation to implement them.

Embrace failure. No matter what happens in the course of your journey toward success, never consider yourself a failure. One of the greatest problems people have with failure is that they are too eager to criticize certain situations in their lives and label them as failures. But don't lose sight of the forest for the trees. It is how you handle these experiences that matter; they forge you and make you stronger and more prepared for what is to come.

Be self-motivated. Another essential ingredient for success is the ability to inspire and motivate oneself. Self-motivation, often known as internal motivation, involves both the mind and the body. In the conceptual phase, you see yourself as being where you ultimately want to be; in the physical phase, you put forth actual effort toward that goal. Inspiring others to take action—not just any action, but the kind of action you want them to take—is the whole essence of motivation. To achieve your goals in life, you must be proactive, commit yourself fully to your vision of success, and challenge yourself to take action right now.

Best people. You need to be around individuals with the most positive and great minds you can find if you want to achieve your full potential in life. You may tap into the divine force of agreement by surrounding yourself with like-minded people. When judged by the norm, mediocre is regarded as superb. Today is the day to overcome the obstacles you've been facing, and you shouldn't judge your achievement based on what others have or haven't accomplished. You are no better off than the average person if you believe you are doing better than them.

DO NOT START THE NEXT CHAPTER BEFORE COMPLETING THE ASSIGNMENT BELOW

4 steps to help hold yourself ACCOUNTABLE

Step One: Identity what you want (Goals)

_____

_____

_____

_____

What is your vision? WHY Do you want to accomplish this goal?

_____

_____

_____

Step Two: Choose an achievable time frame to accomplish your goals as well as measurable details (what does the result look like?) so you know exactly when you've achieved them.

Goal: _____

Date of Completion: _____ / _____ / _____

Make sure your time frame is achievable.

Set yourself up for success!

Goal: _____

Date of Completion: _____ / _____ / _____

Make sure your time frame is achievable.

Set yourself up for success!

Goal: _____

Date of Completion: _____ / _____ / _____

Make sure your time frame is achievable.

Set yourself up for success!

Goal: _____

Date of Completion: _____ / _____ / _____

Make sure your time frame is achievable.

Set yourself up for success!

Goal: _____

Date of Completion: _____ / _____/ _____

Make sure your time frame is achievable.

Set yourself up for success!

Step Three: Continue to break big steps into smaller and smaller steps until your goals seem less difficult and achievable. Benchmarks are a great way to keep you on track and keep you motivated to keep going. You may find you are moving more quickly or slowly than you expected. That's not a problem. You can adjust!

Example: Big Step: Start Merchandise Business
To Little Step: Create Shopify Account

Big Step _____

To Little Step _____

Big Step _____

To Little Step _____

Big Step _____

To Little Step _____

Step Four: Set up rewards along the way. How will you celebrate once you've reached your goal? Enjoy the journey. Reward yourself with ice cream, cookies, or any fun treat at the end of every day—ONLY if you have accomplished all your Daily Goals!

Rewards: _____

_____

_____

Chapter 8

Use your mind like a Parachute, **It works better when it's OPEN**

You are going to take 100% responsibility for your life if you want to design the life of your dreams. That entails giving up all of your justifications, victim narratives, explanations for why you can't or why you haven't thus far, and all of your external cause-and-effect arguments.

You have to abandon them all permanently. The past has passed. Who is to be blamed? It makes no difference. All that matters is for you to decide to take action moving ahead as though you are solely accountable for everything that does or does not happen to you.

You need to task your brain and be responsible for yourself. "How did I create that?" if things didn't go as planned. Why did I think like that? What did I think? What have I said or not said? What did I do or fail to do to cause that outcome? How did I influence the behavior of the other person? What must I do differently the next time to achieve the desired outcome?

In a success compound, only the strongest survive. Not necessarily physically strong but resilient and mentally strong people. It's normal to feel stuck on a plateau at times, but remember that this is just a temporary setback. Don't worry; feeling like this is completely normal. It's just a part of the journey towards success. The only way you ever get to see the other side is "you have to be resilient to grow."

Remember that every step you take, every obstacle you overcome, is bringing you closer to your ultimate destination. Embrace the challenges and keep pushing forward. You are capable of achieving greatness, and this is just one small step toward your success.

Remember, No Excuse; You are Getting This Done! Take a deep breath, trust in yourself, and keep moving forward with determination and positivity. The journey may be tough, but you are tougher. Keep going! You know what? Everything in the past has actually been perfect! Every experience, every challenge, every obstacle has led you to this very moment.

Don't give up when you feel tired of pushing. But you can rest. Keep going, and remember that success is just around the corner. You have the strength and determination to overcome any obstacle that comes your way. Believe in yourself and keep pushing forward towards your goals. Don't be discouraged by the slow progress. Success takes time and effort, but it will come if you stay focused and determined. Your dream is within reach, and with perseverance and determination, you will achieve it. You've got this!

The best action is to start your journey!

BE WILLING TO BE A BEGINNER EVERY SINGLE MORNING

...GROWTH MINDSET

Developing a growth mindset is a belief that our abilities can be developed and that we can constantly learn. It is based on the knowledge that intelligence is not a finite and fixed quality but rather something that can increase with effort and experience.

I read an article about how to develop a growth mindset. This article explains the importance of having a growth mindset in order to succeed and grow as a person. I do not think many people realize that they have the potential to do just anything that they put their minds to. We are rather stuck with our limitations, and we are afraid to take action. We just feel that we are limited to only the things that we are capable of doing without getting out of our comfort zone. These are major signs of a fixed mindset.

Research made with students also suggests that those who have a growth mindset can perform better in their tests through learning and hard work than those who are merely intelligent. This shows that a growth mindset is an open mind to all possibilities of success.

USE YOUR MIND LIKE A PARACHUTE; IT WORKS BETTER WHEN IT'S OPEN!

To get better, you have to be willing to learn from your mistakes and always find new ways how to improve.

Have you ever felt like you are not smart enough in a particular field of interest? As if you are not talented enough to pursue your passion? Or maybe you were discouraged from starting up a project because people questioned your capability? This is when you would need a growth mindset the most!

IF YOU KEEP DOING WHAT YOU HAVE BEEN DOING, YOU WILL KEEP GETTING WHAT YOU HAVE BEEN GETTING... GOOD OR BAD!

If you're struggling to make decisions, give yourself a timeline. For example, you might choose to limit your overwhelm by saying, "I must pick by 'x' deadline." This can help you regain control and reduce the feeling of mental paralysis. A golden nugget to *commit* to memory says,

"Do great things, and great people will find you."

Take your existing problems and solve them in a new way! There is always a better and different way to solve a problem. Let your creativity soar free. Free that bird from its cage. Launch for the wind. With a different approach, you can discover new opportunities and learn things about yourself. Remember that problem-solving is an ongoing process, and there may be multiple solutions to a single problem. Refuse to box your mind; it isn't *pizza*.

DON'T BE AFRAID TO STEP OUTSIDE THE BOX AND BUILD YOUR OWN BOX!

DO NOT START THE NEXT CHAPTER BEFORE UNDERSTANDING AND COMPLETING THE ASSIGNMENT BELOW.

Here are questions that can help you embrace the growth mindset.

How often do you learn something new?

_____

One of the characteristics of having a growth mindset is that you have the opportunity to learn as often as possible. *How often do you ask for help?*

_____

With a growth mindset, you will not hesitate to ask for help when you need it. You would not be afraid of what people would think about you asking for help because your main aim is to learn, develop and improve.

How often do you take up challenging tasks?

_____

If you want to develop a growth mindset, you must dare yourself to do things that you have been afraid of doing the things that you have never done before. All these experiences will boost your exposure to growth.

Chapter 9

Journaling Your Journey

Journaling is like a workout for your brain. It's a mental exercise that helps put your brain on steroids in a good way.

When you journal, you're engaging both the left and right hemispheres of your brain. The left hemisphere is responsible for logical thinking, while the right hemisphere is responsible for creativity and imagination. By bringing these two hemispheres together, you're tapping into your full brain power and opening your mind to limitless think-ing.

"TAKE TIME TO JOURNAL! WRITING CONNECTS TO THE BRAIN THAT HELPS OPEN YOUR MIND TO LIMITLESS THINKING"

Plus, journaling is a great way to organize your thoughts and ideas. It's like creating a roadmap for your brain. You can jot down your goals, brainstorm new ideas, and track your progress. It's like having a personal assistant for your brain.

And let's not forget the mindfulness and self-awareness benefits of journaling. When you take the time to reflect on your thoughts and emotions, you're giving your brain a chance to process and make sense of things. It's like hitting the mental reset button and clearing out the clutter in your brain.

So, grab a pen and paper (or your favorite journaling app, we're not picky) and start flexing your brain muscles. Who knows, maybe you'll come up with the next big idea that changes the world. Or maybe you'll just have a really cool doodle of a unicorn. Either way, it's a win-win.

Chapter 10

Your Dream, Your Purpose in Life

Many people spend their whole lives trying to realize their purpose, only to be left with nothing once they finally get there. Some people give up on their dreams before they even begin. Following your dreams is important, but you need determination and perseverance to follow your dreams. It's not for the weak of the heart. You should expect opposition from all quarters. Both those closest to you and strangers will waste no time in informing you why your plan is, at best, foolish and, at worst, impossible. It might be nerve-wracking to risk safety for an uncertain destination. Safety is nice, but it's not exactly thrilling.

Here are a dozen good reasons why you should stop making excuses and go to work on that goal you've been putting off.

Courage comes from following your dreams.

Even if you don't feel very brave right now, taking that leap of faith and going forward to pursue your goals is the first of many actions that will help you gain courage. Success comes as you take steps toward realizing your goals. Every victory, no matter how large or small, produces more victories. The confidence you gain from these victories will allow you to take on even more challenging endeavors.

Dreaming big forces you to face your fears and learn from your mistakes.

How often have you allowed fear to prevent you from going after what you want? Trying to avoid disappointment? Don't you like transitions? Worried about accomplishing your goals? Fear paralyzes and destroys hope.

Live extreme and push your boundaries. Why? Simply because there will be no other time for you to do this. I don't care if your legs are too tight to lift that weight. Break through that barrier and create new ones.

IT'S NEVER OVER UNLESS YOU QUIT...AND QUITTING IS NOT AN OPTION!!

What's stopping you? Are you too tired? Don't have enough time! Excuses sound best to the person who's making them up. Stop feeling sorry for yourself. You've got a problem with your life? Recognize that those excuses aren't valid; they are only fabricated. They are lies, and how do you stop the lie? You stop them with the truth.

Pursuing your passions helps you stay focused on what's most important in life.

A person's deepest desires are usually congruent with their most important beliefs. There may be a lot of upheavals and stress in your life. There will always be reasons you don't have the time or energy to go after your goals.

This also will pass once you begin rearranging your schedule and devoting your efforts to achieving your goals. You start to realize that your aspirations reflect your core beliefs. Pursuing your goals will help you prioritize them more clearly.

Following your passions motivates those around you.

Others may find confidence in you as you push towards following your dreams and purpose in life. Many people are like salmon swimming upstream; they do not consider going against the tide until they encounter someone else doing so. Following your passions goes against the norm. You will attract attention when you break with convention in pursuit of a more glorious and accomplished life.

Ignore the opinions of others and work toward your goals. The dreamers around you will likely take note of your progress and start encouraging you. Your courage will most often encourage other people to follow their dreams.

WE ALL HAVE THE SAME 24 HOURS IN A DAY; WHAT ARE YOU DOING WITH YOURS?

Chasing your dream helps you discover yourself and your true potential.

Following one's passion can be a wonderful journey of self-discovery. You learn what you're capable of and discover your own identity. Following your passion will force you to confront your limitations and show you where you've set the bar for yourself.

On the path to realizing your dream, you'll encounter obstacles and challenges, but you'll also uncover strengths and abilities you didn't know you had. Following your passions can teach you as much about yourself as traveling can teach you about the world.

The more you work toward pursuing your goals, the more possibilities open up to you. More realistic expectations motivate more ambitious pursuits. Realizing your full ability makes the opinions of others less important, and the walls and limits that society built to keep you inside crumble. You soon start to live an unconventional and flourishing lifestyle.

Dreaming keeps you optimistic while you pursue them.

Dreamers have boundless hope. A dreamer's drive comes from the belief that one day they will realize their vision. One goes from being a dreamer to a doer when they keep working toward their goals and never gives up on their hopes for the future.

Pursuing your goals is a true test of determination.

Not experiencing success is not the murderer of dreams; rather, it is the inability to progress. On the road to achieving their goals, every dreamer encounters a number of setbacks and disappointments. Being able to keep going when things get tough is what separates the dreamers from the achievers. Without tenacity, success in life is impossible.

THE ROAD TO SUCCESS IS ALWAYS UNDER CONSTRUCTION!!!

Following your passions is an inspiration to your kids.

Children forget everything you tell them. "What you are stays with them forever." Jim Henson

When you're an adult, you can be anybody or whatever you choose to be. Isn't that what we teach kids over and over again? Is it more effective to tell your children that anything is possible or actually demonstrate to them that anything is possible? The best way to inspire your children and others to follow their dreams is to follow your own.

Never look back with remorse if you follow your passions.

Too many people spend their lives trying to please other people rather than pursuing their own happiness. Don't accept anything less than the life you envision for yourself, no matter how nice or great it may be. Your dreams are unique to you, and you alone will have to bear the weight of the regret that comes with not pursuing them.

If you allow distractions from everyone around you, you'll get off your purpose, waste your time, waste money, and chase unnecessary stuff. The best thing you can do is to discipline yourself and stay on your own with your timing. You don't have to cut off your friends, but there's a time when if you choose a different path, you have to distance yourself.

EVERYONE THAT COMES WITH YOU CAN'T GO WITH YOU!

SOMETIMES PEOPLE HAVE TO GET OFF THE ELEVATOR ON YOUR WAY TO THE TOP FLOOR.

It's possible that certain chances you take won't pay off. You may fail spectacularly. But you know what definitely won't occur? There will be no regrets as you get older.

Pursuing one's passions guarantees a fascinating existence.

Anything is possible when you take risks and go after your goals. An adventurous existence is one in which the future is a blank slate, and the options are as many as grains of sand on a beach. There's no such thing as a risk-free experience, but there are plenty of benefits to be had by taking a chance on something new.

Pursuing one's ambitions is a path to discovering one's true calling.

Each of us has brilliance, just like a child does. We were given life to reveal the divine greatness already present within us. Everyone has it; it's not limited to a select few. And when we let our brilliance show, we unwittingly encourage others to do the same. As we let go of our anxiety, we make the world a better place for those around us.

Pursue your passions and make every day count.

Following your passions requires you to be yourself and put yourself and your values first. Living a life free of remorse. It's the kind of existence that motivates others to take the plunge themselves. The light you shed by summoning your strength in the face of setbacks and anxiety will help others find their own way. The decision to quit seeking mediocrity and begin seeking one's aspirations is a spark that can start a fire and illuminate the world.

Begging will not get you where you want to go. You have to be willing to PUT IN THE WORK!

What I mean is that you won't get far in life if you rely on other people to fund your desires and fulfill your goals. You are responsible for making them come true.

Important things to know about dreams

Below are a few things you should probably know about dreams to give you an edge and also more reasons why you should keep pursuing that dream of yours.

Vision Is Very Specific. Only you know exactly how your dreams appear and feel. Others do not share your vision or ambition. Depending on others will put you in a position where you are working for other people's aspirations and objectives rather than your own.

Don't expect people to comprehend what you're trying to do.

They demand results right away. You can clearly see this when people hear about your dreams for the first time, and almost immediately, their reaction is negative; they call you all kinds of stuff (like crazy, daydreamer, and so on) and try to make you quit. They really don't understand your vision because it's specific to who you are.

NEVER SHARE YOUR DREAMS WITH DREAM KILLERS!

Hard Work is necessary. Now you need to have the correct plan in place to reach your goals. This is critical, and it might take some time to figure out what works. Yet once you know that hard work is required. It's time to get to work, and here is where highly clever individuals lose to those who are willing to work, work, and work some more. Everybody wants to be great, but only a few are willing to slep up to that moment and take action.

NON-SUCCESSFUL PEOPLE HIT A BRICK WALL AND QUIT!!!

SUCCESSFUL PEOPLE HIT A BRICK WALL AND FIGURE OUT HOW TO GO AROUND IT, UNDER IT, OVER IT, OR THROUGH IT!!!

When you fantasize about achieving anything, there is a gap between where you are now and where you want to be in a few months. The gap can be immense; there is no limit to it. Ideas and plans tell you what you need to do to get there, but doing what you need to do requires a tremendous amount of effort!

Your dream is counting on you. PUSH! Just push past the pain. PUSH! You will feel discouraged sometimes and face obstacles, but be ready to face them.

The truth is that you are equipped with every resource, willpower, and knowledge. If you want it, TAKE IT! It's time to make it happen.

WHEN YOU HAVE DONE ALL THAT YOU CAN DO.....DO MORE!!!!

Day after day, you must fill that need. It demands a significant amount of effort and dedication. You may know what you need to do, but in order to execute it consistently, you must establish a strong willingness to work hard no matter what.

I AM! I CAN! I WILL!

That's what makes all the difference.

When you're truly invested in something, no amount of adversity or opposition can make you give up.

Everyone will have an opinion about what you're doing, and some may attempt to convince you to give up. Nevertheless, as I already indicated, they don't comprehend the degree to which you're doing it in the first place. Secondly, they could be envious of you. BEWARE OF FAKE FRIENDS!

EVERYONE THAT'S IN YOUR CIRCLE
IS NOT IN YOUR CORNER!!!

We all have this need to feel like we're making progress in life. When we see other people working hard to get something better, it makes us feel jealous and angry. It's natural to feel left behind when they're making progress, and you're not.

When someone dismisses your dream, the greatest thing you can do is just not care!

This method really works for me; it calms me down and lets me focus on my goals without any distractions. That's exactly right—don't care about their thoughts since there's no compelling reason to do so. Your dreams and goals are more powerful than gossip and idle talk. Don't waste time fighting the next time someone dismisses your dream. Say "Fine" and go about your business.

You Do Not Have Eternity.

You can have a wonderful vision, a genuine enthusiasm for it, be devoted to working hard, and be laser-focused, but you must recognize that goals must be met within a certain timeframe.

I'm not trying to put you under pressure, but you don't have to keep dreaming; just swing into action. Just like in an entry-level job, you will learn on the job, and everything will soon become clearer.

Sometimes people have fantastic ideas. They start implementing them for real, the effects start to appear, and then they quit. It's time to unwind a bit. The difficulty is that a tiny wait becomes a huge pause, outcomes deteriorate as a result, and you begin to think, "Is it really worth it?"

Yes, of course! That's why you set clear goals and objectives for your life—because you really wanted them.

You can take a break, but don't stop. Laziness is contagious.

The important takeaway here is that you must set a start date and a deadline for every goal you want to achieve.

What tasks must you complete this week, month, and year to move you closer to your goals? Keep track of your outcomes on a weekly basis; this will motivate you to keep striving to achieve more and more without pausing to reflect on your job.

Compete with yourself: if you got X amount of money last week, see if you can double it next week, quadruple it next month, and so on. Do you see what I mean?

I mentioned money, but it may be whatever you want to attain. Gather some measurements and set a challenge for yourself to multiply those values. Get yourself closer to your objective.

You don't have forever to complete it; the ideal moment to begin is right now!

Call to action

1.   Create a visual representation of your dreams.

Our larger life goals form the basis of all of our dreams. Hence, if you find yourself setting goal after goal and making little progress, it's possible that you're running away from your big dream and pursuing goals that aren't really in line with them.

Constantly be on the hunt for

who you have not become yet!

The first step in setting new goals is to make a picture of these high goals and my ideal future. This phase may also involve considering your values and what is essential to you.

2. Define your dreams and identify your goals.

Make your dreams and goals as definitive and specific as possible. Create a list of dreams you want to accomplish and a congruent list of goals. These goals might be distant in the future or something you can attain in the next few months. Make sure they release you, regardless of the timeline.

3. Create an action plan.

"A goal without a plan is just a wish."

It is advisable that, while you have a concrete idea of what your dreams and goals are, you develop a course of action by which you will be achieving them. Plan out the precise actions you'll take, the time you'll devote each week, and the days you'll work on them.

The ability to track your development is another crucial aspect of this. Create a method to help you determine whether or not your action plan is effective for you and what changes need to be made.

4. Write down your goals daily.

Writing down your goals can boost your mental awareness and the need to meet them. It is capable of making you feel motivated to work toward your dreams each day.

5. Develop a positive NO EXCUSES GET IT DONE mindset.

Make sure the thoughts that occupy your mind are positive and empowering ones. Every day, make it a habit to always have positive thoughts that align with achieving your set goals.

Chapter 11

THE MONEY Chapter

Secrets on How to Build Generational Wealth

"IT'S NOT ABOUT HOW MUCH YOU MAKE; IT'S ABOUT HOW MUCH YOU KEEP."

Almost every individual on planet Earth wants to be rich and wealthy. The currency to reach this objective is time, work, and discipline. You will have to always resist the temptation to follow the dangerous paths offered by get-rich-quick schemes and possibilities that seem too good to be true.

Becoming wealthy is possible; you only need to follow certain principles and strategies to be able to achieve this feat. A lot of people complain about wages being stagnant. Truly, wages can be stagnant, but when you look deeply, it is only stagnant on people who are stagnant. There's no reason for you to be stuck somewhere because something that was out of your control didn't work out. You can't control the uncontrollable, but you CAN control how you react to it.

The catch is the earlier you realize and start putting them into practice, the better your chances of success. Before going deeply into that, there are numerous ways in which the rich and the poor perspective differ. Not only can you see it in their actions, but you'll also observe that the way they think about making money affects how they speak, see, and comprehend everything else they perceive.

The best way to help the poor

is to not be one of them!

The poor are concerned with survival, while the rich are concerned with having more than enough.

Everyone has an explanation for their actions, but the poor take it to an extreme. They have a valid reason for their actions, which is to ensure their survival until what comes next. This way of thinking affects their work ethic, as they would rather obtain a simple job that pays them fast so that they can survive in the short term than construct structures that ensure a steady flow of income. They do not consider the long-term or consistency, so they do not invest in themselves or their surroundings in order to create something that will endure.

The poor consider the addition, while the wealthy expand.

We learned in mathematics that addition and multiplication are distinct operations. This best illustrates the contrast between those who are poor and the rich. When a poor person is given the same quantity of resources as a wealthy person, the poor person will rather add things up to make at least a reasonable profit. The wealthy individual, on the other hand, prefers to continue investing his capital until he has created a system that generates a steady stream of income with the same quantity of capital.

POOR PEOPLE WANT TO LOOK RICH!

RICH PEOPLE WANT TO BE RICH!!

The poor rely on their instinct, whereas the rich prepare beforehand.

People frequently fail to recognize that a plan is distinct from a strategy. A plan is what you intend to do, while a strategy is how you intend to do it. In other words, a strategy is a procedure that ensures a task is completed regardless of the circumstances. Everyone is expected to devise a plan for every task that must be completed. But the poor appear to find it simple to make plans without a strategy to achieve the desired outcomes. Therefore, they are limited because they act based on their instincts and emotions rather than a solid plan for completing tasks.

The poor see money as a reward, whereas **the rich see it as an investment.**

Money is only as significant as you deem it to be. Money is never a necessity, but the poor tend to believe otherwise. To clarify, money is a tool that assists you to acquire what you require. And because of that, it's less important than what you need. If you get this wrong, your goals will be off. The implication is that money is not the end product; rather, it is a means to an objective.

MONEY IS WORTHLESS UNTIL IT IS PUT TO WORK!

The poor think of a problem, while the rich think of a solution.

In today's society, the importance of problem-solving skills continues to rise. Whether at work, with their families, in school, or for recreation, people want to get tasks done. The majority of the time, they do not care how things are done; they only care that they come out correctly. The result is recognized, but the problem is not. People who only identify issues are not commended for this reason. No one receives credit for pointing out a job's flaws; credit is given to those who propose viable solutions. When the poor are given a mission, they see not only the problems that affect them but also those that are likely to affect the completion of the task. In contrast, the rich see every employment as an opportunity. Not only do they search for potential problems, but they also devise solutions for the problems they identify.

To better understand wealth, you need to understand these principles and strategies.

- Saving and investing
- Setting goals and making plans
- Investing in education and skills
- Managing debts
- Paying off debts.... By The Way, There is such a thing as GOOD DEBT!!!
- Learning the importance of taxes and their effect on you. Instead of complaining about why the wealthy (1%) does not pay lots of taxes, learn how this is done LEGALLY!
- Building a strong credit history. Your CREDIT can be your investment. Credit Education is crucial. Take the time and learn how to maintain excellent credit.

This chapter will talk about how all these principles work and how they can best help you create and manage wealth.

You are paid based on the problems you can solve!!
What you should start with is earning money. While it may seem so simple and basic, this stage is the most important for people who are just getting started. There are a lot of resources online that show why it's important to save money and how a small amount of money saved regularly over time and allowed to compound can grow into a large

amount of money. However, these resources never explain how to start saving money in the first place.

Earned income and passive income are the two main methods of earning money. Earned money is earned from your job, while passive income comes from investments. However, the latter would only be possible after you have saved enough to invest from your paid income.

"WEALTHY PEOPLE SAVE 75% OF THEIR INCOME AND THEN USE THAT MONEY TO CREATE "CASH FLOW" AND "PASSIVE INCOME."

The following inquiries may help you decide what you want to accomplish and where your earned money will come from if you are either starting a career or thinking about changing careers:

What interests you? By engaging in work that you like and find meaningful, you will perform better, develop a career that will last longer, and increase your chances of financial success. According to one study, more than 90% of employees stated they would swap a portion of their career earnings for a job with more purpose.

What do you excel at? Consider your strengths and how you may utilize them to support yourself by getting a job that you would find relatively easy to do.

What will be lucrative? Choose occupations that fit what you excel at and love doing and will fulfill your financial goals.

Getting there? Find out what education, experience, and training you need to have in order to get your desired job.

Taking these considerations into account can help set you quickly on the right path toward achieving your goal.

Another important thing you might or must do to maximize your earning potential is to invest in your education and skills. Getting advanced academic degrees, industry-specific certificates, and training programs are all useful for building your human capital.

Set Goals and Develop a Plan. Defining your financial goals would make the whole process of saving a lot easier. Do you aim to fund your retirement, maybe an early retirement? Is it towards funding your kids' education? Buying a house, maybe a second one? Or saving money to start your own company. Whatever you aim to achieve, it is imperative that you have clear and well-written goals.

Scared money doesn't make money!

Be smart with your money but don't be scared to take risks!

The next step is to develop a strategy or strategies that will ensure you achieve your set out desired financial goals. This includes setting up a budget to encourage you to save more money, boosting your income via education or professional progression, or making investments in long-term growth prospects. You need to have a written plan for the budget. No one accidentally wins at anything, and you are not an exception. Without a written plan on how to spend your money, you are going to lose. Your strategy should be practical, adaptable, and long-term-oriented. Review your progress often, and don't be afraid to make changes when necessary to stay on course.

There are 3 types of income you must have:

1. **EARNED:** This comes from traditional employment.
2. **PORTFOLIO:** This comes from investments such as stocks and bonds.
3. **PASSIVE:** This is generated through assets that produce cash flow, such as rental properties or businesses. Passive income is often the least

taxed because it's generated through assets that can produce tax deductions and other benefits

KEEP CONTROL OF YOUR MONEY!!! After you have set out your financial goals, it is recommended you start taking action toward them, such as saving. Save money for both short-term and long-term goals. Several experts advise having three to six months' salary saved up.

BONUS TIP: Don't save all of your money in a savings bank account. Invest in smart assets so your money can work for you.

Track your spending monthly. A compact, pocket-sized notepad might work well for this, although you might wish to utilize financial software. Keep a record of every purchase you make, no matter how tiny; more often than not, individuals are shocked to discover where all of their money goes.

Try cutting out excesses where necessary by breaking down your spending into needs and wants. Needs like clothes, food, and shelter are important. You should also include the cost of health insurance, vehicle insurance if you own a car, and life insurance if you have dependents. Many more expenses will just be wants.

STOP SPENDING YOUR MONEY ON STUPID STUFF... UNTIL YOU HAVE ENOUGH WEALTH TO SPEND YOUR MONEY ON STUPID STUFF!

Make a savings target. Try to stick to your budget after you've determined how much you can save each month. This does not imply that you must always be thrifty or live simply. Be free to reward yourself and sometimes spend (in a suitable amount) if your savings objectives are being met. You'll feel better and have more drive to continue on your path.

Automate your savings. Having your company or bank set up an automatic transfer of a certain amount of each paycheck into a different savings or investing account is a simple method that ensures you save a specific amount each month. Similarly to this, you may contribute to your employer's 401(k) or another retirement plan by having money automatically deducted from your income.

Find high-yield savings. One of the best ways to be sure you are saving enough is to set a spending budget. Cut back on excess and unnecessary spending and put that money in the bank instead. **Ok, STOP!** I don't want to confuse you... YES, keep your money in the bank during the saving phase, but THEN use those same savings to IN-

VEST or start your business. Also, you will need to keep enough money in the bank for your everyday living expenses: Rent, Mortgage, Car, Groceries, Bills, Gas, etc. I hope that clears up any confusion.

Go for savings accounts with the highest interest rates and the lowest fees to maximize the return on your funds. If you have the financial means to lock away your money for many months or years, certificates of deposit (CDs) may be an excellent choice for your savings.

BONUS TIP: Precious Metals may be a good option for saving your money (Silver & Gold). Meaning, Convert some of your cash into Silver and Gold. It can always be converted back when needed. Silver and Gold will always hold more value than Cash or the U.S. Dollar.

But keep in mind that cost-cutting is relatively effective. When you live less than you make and get out of debt, you can save some money. The truth remains that you are going to be broke till you start saving some money. You have to fix your life with what's working for you. You should consider measures to improve your revenue if your expenses are already really low.

"TAKE HOW MUCH INCOME YOU GENERATE PER YEAR AND DIVIDE IT BY 365. THAT AMOUNT IS HOW MUCH YOU MAKE PER DAY. IF YOU ARE NOT HAPPY WITH YOUR DAILY RATE, THEN DOUBLE YOUR EFFORT. IF YOU WANT TO 10X YOUR INCOME, THEN 10X YOUR EFFORT.

Setting a spending limit is one of the best strategies to ensure that you are saving enough money. Reduce your unnecessary and extra expenditures and invest your savings instead.

The next step after managing to save some money is to invest it so that it will grow with interest. Savings are crucial, but bank account interest rates are often quite low, and your money runs the danger of losing value over time due to inflation. One day you will be able to purchase anything you want if you put your money to work for you.

Never invest in anything you don't understand! Learn, then make your decision!

For new investors (or generally any investor), diversification is perhaps the most effective method. To put it simply, you should try to diversify your investment portfolio. That's because investments perform differently with time. For instance, bonds may be offering strong returns if the stock market is experiencing a losing stretch. However, if Stock A is struggling, Stock B can be doing really well.

Mutual funds have some built-in diversification because they invest in a wide range of securities. Also, investing in both a stock fund and a bond fund (or many stock funds and multiple bond funds, for example) rather than just one of the two will increase your diversification.

Another generalization is that investment is very suitable for young adults, as you can afford to take more risks while you're younger since you'll have more time to make up for any losses.

NEVER INVEST IN ANYTHING YOU DON'T UNDERSTAND! IF YOU KNOW ABOUT INTEREST, YOU WILL MAKE IT; IF YOU DON'T KNOW, YOU WILL PAY IT!

Spend some time learning about the different types of investments if you aren't already familiar with them. Despite the wide variety of investment options available, the majority of investors often choose to start with stocks, bonds, and mutual funds.

Stocks are a representation of a company's own shares. When you purchase stock, you become a minor shareholder in that company and will get to enjoy benefits from the rise in both its share price and any dividends it may pay. Bonds are often thought of as being less risky than stocks; however, the risk associated with stocks may vary greatly from firm to firm.

Bonds function similarly to government or corporate IOUs. When you purchase a bond, the issuer pledges to return your funds, together with interest, at a later time. Bonds are often seen as being less risky than stocks but with fewer benefits. Bond-rating organizations also issue letter grades to bonds based on their level of risk by assigning letter grades.

Mutual funds are collections of securities, often consisting of stocks, bonds, or a mix of the two. Shares in mutual funds give you access to some portion of the whole pool. The risk of mutual funds varies as well, depending on the investments they make.

Exchange-traded funds (ETFs) are similar to mutual funds in that each share contains the whole of a portfolio of assets. But ETFs are listed on exchanges and traded similarly to stocks. Certain exchange-traded funds (ETFs) follow significant stock indices like the S&P 500, specific industrial sectors, or asset classes like bonds and real estate.

BONUS TIP: Additionally, always be in the business of providing the three basic needs of man.

- **Cement/concrete** (shelter/real estate),
- **Food**
- **Textile** (clothing).

Any business that keeps this type of focus will flourish! Land and Precious Metals are forms of money! Do not allow external factors to dictate your financial decisions.

Be sure you have enough savings and money left over to manage any unforeseen financial problems before you begin investing.

Stop spending money on stuff you don't need! Protect Your Assets

You put a lot of effort into earning your money and building your fortune. The worst scenario is losing everything in the case of a sudden catastrophe or unanticipated circumstance. Your home may burn down in a fire, you might get injured in a vehicle accident, and you might lose out on future income if you pass away too soon.

Since it shields you against these and other risks, insurance is a crucial element of creating wealth. In the event of a fire, home insurance will rebuild your house and possessions, vehicle insurance will make you whole after a collision, and life insurance will pay your dependents in the event of an early death. Another kind of coverage that will replace your income in the event that you become injured, ill, or otherwise unable to work is long-term disability insurance. Although insurance policies tend to cost more as you age, even young, healthy individuals should think about buying them. This implies that purchasing life insurance today, even if you are 25 years old and unmarried, may be much more affordable than doing so when you are 10 years older and have a spouse, children, and a mortgage.

BONUS TIP: Whole Life Insurance could be a "Game-Changer" for you as well.

Minimize the Impact of Taxes.

SUPER BONUS TIP:

- **Tax Evasion** is Illegal. (Don't Do This)
- **Tax Avoidance** is LEGAL (This is the #1 strategy on how the wealthy stays wealthy)
- Find a Very Good **"Tax Strategist"** who understands the Tax Avoidance laws. You will thank me later.

Paying taxes may hinder your attempts to save enough; this is true and often disregarded. Of course, when we earn and spend money, we are all subject to income tax and sales tax, but our investments and assets are also subject to taxation. Knowing your tax risks and coming up with strategies to reduce their consequences are crucial.

Learn the tax laws and real financial education

You would be amazed by how much wealth you would amass by simply understanding the effects of taxes and implementing ways to reduce their impact.

Maintaining a Good Credit Score.

Getting and keeping a good credit score is a key part of building and keeping wealth over the long term. If you have a good credit history and a high credit score, you may get a reduced interest rate and better loan conditions, which can save you hundreds of dollars in interest costs over time.

Pay off bills on time. Your payment history is one of the key elements that determine your credit score. Paying on time helps develop a strong credit score. Even a few days of late payments may have a major negative effect on your credit score.

Keep your credit utilization low. Another significant aspect that influences your credit score is your credit usage, or how much of your available credit you are really utilizing. You should try to keep your credit use below 30% of your available credit in order to retain a high credit score.

Monitor your credit report. It's a good practice to routinely check your credit report to ensure that all of the data is correct and up to date. Currently, a number of firms can provide you with a credit report without charging you. It's important to challenge any mistakes you notice on your credit report since they might have a negative influence on your credit score.

Try not to create too many new accounts. Your credit score may be somewhat lowered each time you apply for credit. But keep in mind that you risk having an insufficient credit history if you don't use credit cards or have enough credit lines open. Open a few credit cards and obtain a few loans, but do not go overboard.

You can maintain a good credit score and increase your borrowing power over time by adhering to these guidelines and developing good credit habits.

Should I pay off the debt or invest?

It normally makes sense to pay off high-interest debt before making investments if you have any, such as several credit card balances. Few investments ever provide returns as high as credit card fees. After your debt is paid off, use that additional cash toward savings and investments. As much as you can, strive to pay off the whole sum on your credit card each month to prevent accruing interest.

SUPER BONUS TIP:

There is such a thing as **GOOD DEBT!** It's called **OPM** (Other People's Money), Banks, Private Lenders, etc....

This takes lots of discipline, but when you learn how to perfect this strategy, You will be on your way to creating Generational Wealth. The Banks will become your best friend and start throwing money at you because you have created TRUST-worthy relationships with the banks.

Oh Yea, speaking of TRUST....

Here is another **SUPER BONUS TIP:**

As you build your wealth, create a **Family TRUST** to protect all of your assets and to protect YOU. Always remember, You **DON'T** want to own anything, but you **DO** want to **CONTROL** everything. Talk to a TRUST Expert to learn more.

Chapter 12

Maintain Focus and Balance

Distractions are a huge factor in your success, and you sure cannot get over that if you don't understand how important your time is and maintaining a balance in all you do. Achieving a high success rate has a lot to do with being focused and disciplined. Sometimes, you need more effort in this and not that, sometimes more time in that and not this. Most importantly, your success is dependent on your effort in juggling competing priorities.

It's a perpetual balancing act between competing demands on your time. While trying to strike a better work-life balance, it's up to you to decide which aspects of your life are more important. Especially if you have a job and you want your life also. Most jobs out there will rob you of your precious potential and make your time useless if you aren't careful with how you handle your priorities.

Work-life balance and work-life integration take on various forms for different people because of the diversity of their lives and the fluidity of their duties. Some examples include

- An attorney who makes an effort to disconnect while on vacation
- A boss who limits employee contact and stops answering emails after 6 p.m.
- An employee who arranges their work schedule in such a way that they will have time left to spend with their loved ones.

Maintaining a healthy balance between work and life has been linked to better mental, emotional, and physical health. Several studies have found a link between working too many hours and health problems like insomnia, depression, heavy drinking, diabetes, memory loss, and heart disease. When this occurs, it might be more difficult to maintain a healthy work-life balance, increasing the risk of burnout and other negative outcomes.

For example, research from 2014 showed that after workers had been on the job for a certain number of hours, they became less productive and were more likely to get hurt. Having a good balance between work and life is good for the employee's mental and physical health as well as the company's bottom line. Its importance cannot be overemphasized.

Stress at work ranks as the sixth-leading cause of mortality in the United States. Twenty-five percent of people attribute their stress levels to the demands of their employment. People may feel trapped in this situation, but the reality is that there are several more opportunities out there.

"Money without free time is worthless!"

As you make decisions, you bring harmony to your life. You are the source of your own stress. You're just making things worse if you agree to take on additional work when you don't have the ability to handle it or if you don't delegate work that might be assigned.

You must refrain from agreeing to do unnecessary tasks. Just say **NO.** Don't feel pressured to take on every new request from a colleague or manager. Saying "yes" to everything is a surefire way to destroy your work-life balance.

Instead, make time to work through the available options with the person who made the request. For example, it might be possible to take on a new, urgent task if something on your existing to-do list can be delegated elsewhere.

Do not work during breaks. While working from home can be distracting by personal tasks that need to be done during breaks. It's not uncommon for a half-hour break to develop into a frantic session of housework, laundry, dishwashing, and bill-paying. Instead, take advantage of the time between work sessions to focus on yourself.

You must prioritize your actions. And don't multitask. Focus on doing one thing at a time. Multitasking causes worry and high risks of mistakes. Taking care of yourself is crucial. While you're employed, you'll put in long hours. Exhaustion is a common result. But when you finally get things right by delegating your priorities, things will become more relaxed and fun. You'll be able to relax and enjoy life again.

Maintaining equilibrium improves your resilience in the face of challenging emotions and ideas. Create more equilibrium in your life if you want serenity. You'll have more time to consider your options, and your mind will be clearer. It will also help you cope with your emotions more effectively, rather than storing them up inside and letting them out at the worst possible moment.

When you maintain a healthy balance in your life, you're better able to live in the moment. Most times, it appears like you have a lot of things running through your head at once. Sometimes it's not obvious which ones are crucial. You are with your loved ones, you are thinking about your work—a task that must be completed before the deadline—and you can't seem to enjoy your time.

When you have your priorities sorted and carried out at their designated times, you are able to focus on your job while you are working and on any other things during their designated times.

You would be able to learn to teach your brain to be less anxious and more focused in the moment. Part of having laser focus is learning how to keep the main thing, THE MAIN THING!

Overworking puts a person's health in danger since the effects of chronic burnout and elevated stress are far-reaching. Even when constant fatigue keeps telling the body to slow down, a person grows accustomed to these signals and ignores them for the sake of working for money until he collapses. Do you believe someone who is so stressed out and busy is giving both his professional and personal relationships his all? The answer is simply no. He is unable to keep anyone satisfied, even his boss and those at home, and thus there is constant turmoil around him. Work-life balance is crucial because it promotes a person's physical, emotional, and mental welfare, which in turn increases his productivity and efficiency.

The bright side is that you won't be as worn out, overwhelmed, or irritable when you get home. You can relax without hiding from the world for the rest of the day. You'll be able to keep up a meaningful conversation with others and enjoy fellowship without feeling drained. When you spend time with the people that matter to you, you strengthen your relationships with them and enrich your life.

The best approach to successfully starting your day and seeing it through is to establish daily routines. You'll do more in less time and believe that your day was productive. Healthy routine behaviors gradually develop into positive habits over time.

Tips for improving work-life balance

Below, I've compiled tips for improving your work-life balance. You can begin trying them out one at a time or implement a few at once. Remember that finding an approach that works for you is a process and will take time.

DO NOT START THE NEXT CHAPTER BEFORE COMPLETING THE JOURNAL ASSIGNMENT BELOW

1. Evaluating your present life

To create a new work-life integration that meets your requirements, it is important to take some time to reflect on how the many aspects of your life are influencing one another. Take a moment to reflect on your present work-life balance and how it makes you feel. Consider some of these questions:

- Am I giving my interests enough of my time?
- How much time and effort do I give to the things and people who matter to me?
- Am I still on track to achieve my professional and personal Goals? If not, WHY?

- Where am I experiencing the greatest DEAD-END? What is it about this circumstance that has me feeling this way?

Writing down your reactions to these questions will help you zero in on the areas where you believe the most change is required. In the end, you should be able to see things more clearly after answering these questions.

Journaling your thoughts and feelings can be a good way to identify the areas you feel need the biggest adjustments. Ultimately, these questions should help you gain greater clarity.

2. Double-check your priorities

After you have a better idea of what needs changing, you can start prioritizing those changes.

Them: I don't see you at the club!

Me: I don't see you at the bank!

Here are some questions to ponder:

- Am I devoting enough time and energy to the things that really matter?
- Where do I have room to negotiate? In what areas have I been compromising too much?

- Is there anything I can do to make sure I'm giving my goals and relationships the attention they deserve?
- How do I balance my obligations so that I do not neglect any of them?

3. Managing your time

Now that you know what you value most, whether it's getting ahead professionally by logging long hours at the office or reducing the number of emails you check outside of normal business hours, you can focus on improving your time management skills.

Think about how you're presently spending your time and see whether there's any room for improvement. When new activities arise out of the blue, you may "chunk" your time to concentrate on one area at a time or utilize a matrix approach to define priorities. Spend more time learning the best time management techniques that improve your efficiency and happiness.

4. Define your limits

The first step in effective time management is setting limits. It will be crucial to make your limits known. Be SPECIFIC on how much time you will spend on each item, then STOP and move on to the next item or task. For example, don't exceed the number of hours you have set to hold daily practice for studies, with family, etc.

Physical, emotional, and temporary constraints are the three types of work limits. Limit yourself first, and then work your way up. Practice this, and with time you can be sure never to compromise again.

5. Review, Tweak, and Repeat

Whatever steps you take, it's important to keep in mind that you'll probably need to make adjustments to your work-life balance as time goes on. While making significant adjustments in one's life might take time, it's probable that you'll need to stop and evaluate your progress on a regular basis.

You may even decide that switching careers is in your best interest and decide to get a new professional certification in order to better yourself in your chosen field and have a healthy work-life balance.

It is imperative to note that a decent work-life balance will seem different for each individual.

Finally, the goal is to figure out what a meaningful, full life entails for you. Next, look at your career and schedule to see what real improvements you can make – even the smallest changes will help you feel more satisfied.

Remember that your work-life balance will often vary as you take on new positions and retire from previous ones. Thus, check in with yourself on a frequent basis to ensure that you prioritize what is essential to you. These check-ins might provide an opportunity to reflect on what needs to be changed and to look into resources that can assist you in making those changes.

"Don't let the demands of life hold you back from achieving balance and fulfillment. Follow this guide today and start taking action towards a more harmonious and satisfying life!"

Chapter 13

REST – ReASSIGN – REPEAT

Rest: Get Plenty of Sleep

Reassign: Learn to Delegate (You Don't have to do it all by yourself)

Repeat the above two items daily

Learn Yourself!

If you are a morning person, you may want to complete tasks requiring energy and concentration in the morning. A nocturnal person may wish to complete these tasks in the evening. Map the appropriate activities to the appropriate times and avoid wasting high-value periods.

One key strategy for getting your tasks completed is utilizing the Eisenhower Matrix to organize tasks and determine which should be delegated or eliminated based on their importance and priority. Here is an example of how it appears:

Do: Do this task now.

Decide: Schedule a time to do it.

Delegate: Who can do it for you?

Eliminate: Eliminate it.

According to research, it takes an average of 20 - 25 minutes to resume a task after an interruption. This is why it is essential to focus on one task at a time and resist the urge to multitask.

You need to learn how to leverage and outsource resources effectively so that you can maximize your productivity. You'll want to speed up your productivity as your success in life grows, and efficiency is power. Outsource or automate tasks if at all possible.

Tools like Click Funnels and WordPress, for instance, make it easy to create a website rather than starting from scratch. In a similar vein, freelancers can be found on platforms like Upwork and Fiverr for virtually any task imaginable. Don't let a focus on cost-cutting sideline more important business decisions.

Instead of spending time learning something new just because you happen to need it right now, consider hiring someone who is proficient in that area. There is simply too much to do. Outsourcing is the most efficient way to get things done. That frees you up to concentrate on what really matters.

The benefits to your productivity at work and even your life, in general, will be significantly greater if you incorporate even a small number of these practices into your regular routine.

Clean your Workspace. Maintaining a neat and tidy desk and work area has been shown to increase concentration and productivity. A tidy workspace has been shown to increase productivity by more than 15 percent.

Get into the Habit of Exercising First Thing in the Morning. Develop daily habits that help you get started. Anything from quiet reflection to book reading to physical activity is fair game. Having a set routine first thing in the morning can help you focus and get ready for the day ahead. I personally like to get the hard stuff out of the way early in the morning, like exercising, because our bodies wear down as the day goes on, and we tend to use that tiredness as an EXCUSE to not get something done.

Exercising regularly has been shown to improve sleep quality and speed up response times on problem-solving tasks. I work out 20 to 30 minutes a day. You don't need to spend hours in the gym to produce solid results unless your goal is to become a Body Builder or Professional Athlete.

Prepare the Night Before. Make a list of three to five goals for the next day before you go to sleep every night. They can be as specific as you like, for example, by outlining the structure of an article or the key points of a presentation.

This gives form to the tasks you have ahead the following morning.

Write Down your Thoughts and Systemize them. Have a pen and paper handy so you can jot down ideas as they occur to you. You may write down the thought or action you need to remember this way rather than letting it occupy your mind and divert your attention.

Create the best system that works for you to achieve maximum productivity. As a result, you'll spend less time deciding what to do next, which will boost your performance and productivity both in the workplace and in other areas of your life.

Get Enough Rest. You can't make it through the day without the energy and health benefits that come with a good night's sleep.

The human body is a machine that requires regular periods of rest in order to function at peak efficiency. According to a Harvard study from 2007, not getting enough sleep can lead to erratic behavior, poor performance at work, and a loss of productivity. A good night's sleep can help you make quick, confident decisions in high-stakes situations because it improves memory retention, maintains a positive mood, and sharpens cognitive functioning.

Lack of sleep has been shown to affect our judgment and make us more likely to act impulsively. It makes it more difficult to plan and manage intricate projects. Getting less sleep slows down productivity and makes it harder to meet deadlines.

This explains why people who don't get enough sleep might miss important deadlines or have trouble organizing their schedules so that they have enough time to get everything done.

The 2-Minute Principle. The essence of this rule, as demonstrated by productivity guru David Allen in his best-selling book "Getting Things Done," is to complete a task as soon as possible if you can do so within two minutes. If you put off doing the little things, they will likely hamper your productivity as it usually takes longer to analyze and complete them later. Emails should be answered in batches, notes should be reviewed, lecture recaps watched, follow-ups done, dishes washed, laundry folded, etc.

The benefit of this is that, before you know it, you will have completed these tasks without knowing and will have enough time to spend with your loved ones and engage in other social activities.

DO THE FOLLOWING EVERY DAY!!!

For you to be productive, you have to develop an action plan for each day and strictly follow it. Although you might find it difficult to stick with it initially, soon enough, after consistent and intentional practice, it will become natural to you.

Create a list of tasks for each day.

Create a list of tasks you need to complete in order of priority. By doing so, you make your activities for the day seem less overwhelming and organized in a step-by-step manner. If a given task seems too vague or intimidating, you can further divide it into two or three smaller action items that seem more doable.

Set a timeline for each.

For tasks for which you can estimate the required time for completion, establish a timeframe for completing them. It is essential to create a timeline you can reasonably follow.

Designate resources

As stated earlier in this chapter, automate and outsource some work to experts so that you can concentrate on the major tasks that only you must do.

Monitor the progress

Finally, describe how you will ensure each task in your action plan is completed on time.

Conclusion

The path to conquering mental paralysis and achieving success in life is not an easy one, but it is one that is worth taking. The journey requires mental toughness, resilience, and determination. With the right NO EXCUSES GET IT DONE mindset and strategies, anyone can overcome mental paralysis and achieve their full potential. This Book is your guide to overcoming mental paralysis and achieving success in all areas of life.

Mental paralysis can affect anyone at any point in their life, and it can manifest in different forms, including anxiety, fear, and self-doubt. However, it is possible to overcome mental paralysis and achieve success and happiness in life. In this book, you've learned about the causes and symptoms of mental paralysis, as well as effective strategies to conquer it.

You've explored the various ways in which mental paralysis can negatively impact your life. You've learned to recognize the signs of mental paralysis, such as procrastination, indecision, and fear of failure. Additionally, you've discovered how to overcome these obstacles by developing a growth mindset, setting goals, and taking action.

One of the key takeaways from this book is that mental paralysis is often rooted in our beliefs and thought patterns. By becoming more aware of our thoughts and beliefs, we can learn to identify and challenge negative self-talk and limiting beliefs. This, in turn, can help us to reframe our thoughts and develop a more positive and empowering mindset.

Another important lesson is that taking action is crucial to overcoming mental paralysis. Rather than waiting for the perfect moment or the perfect opportunity, it's important to take small steps towards your goals, even if they feel uncomfortable or uncertain at first. By taking action, you can build momentum, develop resilience, and gain the confidence you need to achieve your goals.

Remember, **EMBRACE THE GRIND!** If you embrace your struggles, you will have more courage to conquer them when they appear. Enjoy the journey. The journey to-wards overcoming mental paralysis is not always easy, but it is worth it in the end.

Call to action:

Write down the problem, and place it in a visible place, most likely, a place you would be able to see it (In your daily journal or on your wall). You could replicate it by pasting it almost everywhere in your room, alongside the solutions you have presented and how you intend to tack-le this particular problem. Whenever you pass by it, read the words to yourself, more importantly, the solution(s); by doing this, you create a positive mental picture, and your thoughts will begin to shape and form solutions to the problem.

BE EXTREMELY, SUPER CONFIDENT IN WHAT YOU DON'T KNOW!

It may sound counterintuitive at first glance. Howev-er, it highlights the importance of being aware of your own limitations and being honest about what you don't know. Being confident in what you don't know means recognizing that there is always more to learn and that you don't have all the answers. I like to be the **DUMBEST** person in my circle of influence. When you become the SMARTEST, You stop learning. (I use this word DUMB in a positive way in order to make my point... "Never Stop Learning.")

WHEN YOU BUILD AND GROW IN SILENCE, PEOPLE DON'T KNOW WHAT TO ATTACK.

Don't give your haters ammunition to attack and destroy your dream by bragging and running your mouth. Move in silence! Eagles don't fly in flocks! Embrace flying alone sometimes. No one can believe in you more than you! Don't be afraid to jump off the beaten path and start your own journey! Failure is just finding a smarter way to start over! Celebrate every win, no matter how small!

DON'T TELL PEOPLE WHAT YOU ARE GOING TO DO; JUST DO IT AND SHOCK THEM! AFTER YOU SHOCK THEM, STAY SILENT!

ONCE YOU HAVE ACCEPTED YOUR FLAWS, NO ONE CAN USE THEM AGAINST YOU!

BEFORE YOU SPEAK, LISTEN!

BEFORE YOU WRITE, THINK!

BEFORE YOU SPEND, EARN!

BEFORE YOU INVEST, INVESTIGATE!

BEFORE YOU CRITICIZE, WAIT!

BEFORE YOU PRAY, FORGIVE!

BEFORE YOU QUIT, TRY!

BEFORE YOU DIE, GIVE!

DON'T CHASE, ATTRACT!

What belongs to you will find you! This doesn't mean that you should sit back and wait for things to happen to you. Rather, it means that you should focus on what you can control, such as your mindset, skills, and learning. By focusing on building yourself up, developing your skills and passions, and being authentic in your interactions with others, you can naturally attract the people and opportunities that are right for you.

BE CAREFUL WHO YOU TAKE ADVICE FROM.

If they are not where you are trying to go, dismiss their advice unless they are advising you to get advice from an expert who is where you are trying to go. A wise man speaks because he has something to say. A fool speaks because he always has to say something.

God gave us two ears and one mouth for a reason; you will learn more with your mouth closed. Also, when it's time to speak, ask a question.

A TRUE TEAM DOESN'T COMPETE WITH EACH OTHER; THEY "COMPLETE" EACH OTHER!

The best results happen because team members change me to "WE" None of us can achieve greatness on our own; we need one another. Instead of trying to outdo one another or working against each other, team members complement and enhance each other's efforts, resulting in a more effective and efficient outcome.

MCDONALDS IS A REAL ESTATE BUSINESS THAT HAPPENS TO SELL HAMBURGERS.

McDonald's owns many of the properties where its franchises are located, and the company leases these properties to franchisees for a fee. As a result, McDonald's real estate holdings are a significant contributor to its overall profitability and success, making it a key player in the global real estate industry.

OPPORTUNITIES HIDE BEHIND OBSTACLES!

STOP KEEPING BAD COMPANY THAT DISTRACTS YOU! STAY AWAY FROM "STILL" PEOPLE WHO ARE:

- **STILL BROKE!**
- **STILL COMPLAINING!**
- **STILL HATING!**
- **STILL NOWHERE!**

The people we surround ourselves with can have a significant impact on our lives, both positively and negatively.

MOST SUFFER THEIR ENTIRE LIFE BECAUSE THEY ARE NOT WILLING TO SUFFER FROM A FEW UNCOMFORTABLE MOMENTS

Have a crystal clear visualization of what you want! Don't think that you want something; know that you want it! This involves setting specific goals, identifying the steps we need to take to achieve them, and staying focused and committed to our goal.

The first step in breaking the cycle of mental paralysis is to acknowledge that you are experiencing it. This means being honest with yourself about what's going on in your mind and not avoiding or denying the problem.

Set out each day with a renewed resolve to grow, learn, unlearn and relearn as many times as necessary until you become who you want to be. The next step is to understand what causes your mental paralysis. This can be different for everyone, but it's important to identify what situations or thoughts that tend to trigger this feeling for you. In many cases, mental paralysis is caused by perfectionism or the fear of failure.

Try simplifying your life by identifying what's truly important to you and eliminating anything that isn't necessary. This means saying no to social invitations or scaling back on your work commitments. Taking care of yourself physically by eating healthy, exercising regularly, and getting enough sleep will also make it easier for you to make clear-headed decisions.

WAKE UP EVERY DAY BELIEVING THAT YOU ARE GREAT, AND THE NEXT TIME SOMEONE TELLS YOU **"NO, "** FLIP THAT WORD AROUND AND SAY, "IT'S **ON**"! USE THAT WORD "NO" AS MOTIVATION AND MAKE A COMMITMENT TO WIN! HAVING A **NO EXCUSES GET IT DONE** MINDSET WILL FORCE YOU TO WIN

LET'S GOOOOOOOO!

Acknowledgments

To my Best Friend & Biggest Cheerleader, My Beautiful Wife Krystal Denise Turner, aka "Boo Mama"!!!! GOD is Truly Amazing for Blessing me with you. Words Can't express how Amazing you are and how much you mean to me. Let's start with that Billion Dollar Smile that still melts my heart. You are the true essence of the word QUEEN. I am truly blessed to have you as my "Better Half" & Soulmate. I just want to say THANK YOU! I Love You!

Thank you, Mom and Dad, for Raising me to always believe in myself. Who would have thought that this little kid from Detroit would grow up to be an Author? Both of you have always taught me to never Limit myself. Thank You both for sacrificing so much to provide for our family. So many people compliment me on how great of a parent I am, and I always respond by saying THANK YOU. It's because I have two of the greatest parents on earth... I just followed their lead.

"LYRIC & HARMONI, when they say daughters make a father soft and mushy inside, I must agree! Both of you will always be Daddy's little girls. We have been through a lot together... and I hope and pray that I have set a good example for you now that you are both Young Ladies. Both of you will always have a special place in my heart. I Love You!

My Son ROCKY JR. - Words are not enough to express the Love I have for you. I know you are watching my every move... So I ask God every day to Guide My Steps, My Thoughts, My Actions, and My Words. I never understood how a Father could disappear from his son's life and not be bothered. You continue to make me Proud to be your father every day. Don't ever stop being who you are. I Love You, son.

No Excuses - Get It Done!

This portion of the book is the most difficult because there are so many phenomenal people who have been a positive impact on my life. All of You, and you know who you are.... have helped shape and mold me into the man that I am today. It Truly does "Take A Village!" This book would be 1000 pages if I mentioned every one of those awesome individuals. Please don't take it personally if I forget to mention your name. Thank You to My Brother Andre for always believing in me and always challenging me to be the Best! • My Sister for being that protector and safe haven • Dr. Froswa Booker-Drew • Michele Bobadilla • Kate Gardner • Michael Holmes • Pam Gerber • Pastor Thompson & Rev. Hogg • Skip Cheatham The "Vice Squad"- My Ride or Die Brothers and Sisters I grew up with...Shannon Flowers, Derek Jones, James Horton, Rico Brown, Brian Edmond-son, JD Elliby, Eric Green, and Brian Johnson • John Fleming •Reggie D • Lenny Love • Coach Butch McBroom • Coach Gerald Brown • My Stomp Wars Family - I receive so much recognition and praise for creating the Largest Youth Stepping Competition & Movement in the World – but I can't take all of the credit. Stomp Wars would not be where it is today without my amazing Team. Brenda Barlow, Lauren Bridges, Dana Vilardi, Amaya Andujar, Mikaila Montgomery, Marquetta Clayton, Brannon Smith, and every single Volunteer and Judge who has ever served at Stomp Wars. THANK YOU for all of your dedication and hard work.

Rickey Smiley, I am forever grateful to you for providing me with a phenomenal opportunity of joining The Rickey Smiley Morning Show, which has opened up so many doors. I appreciate your friendship, your encouragement, and all of your brotherly advice. I want to thank my entire Rickey Smiley Morning Show Family, Reach Media, and Radio One. Thank You YEA NETWORKS. You can never forget where you've come from, and I must thank K104 FM in Dallas for opening the door to my career in radio.

Printed in the USA
CPSIA information can be obtained
at www.ICGtesting.com
JSHW010334290723
45537JS00003B/10